Suck on the Marrow

D1611503

Suck on the Marrow

poems by

Camille T. Dungy

Red Hen Press | *Los Angeles, CA*

Suck on the Marrow

Library of Congress Cataloging-in-Publication Data

Dungy, Camille T., 1972–
  Suck on the marrow : poems / by Camille Dungy.—1st ed.
    p. cm.
  ISBN 978-1-59709-468-9
  1. Freedmen—Poetry. 2. African Americans—Poetry I. Title.
  PS3604.U538S83 2010
  811'.6--dc22
                    2009036845

The Annenberg Foundation, the James Irvine Foundation, the Los Angeles County Arts Commission, and the National Endowment for the Arts partially support Red Hen Press.

First Edition

Published by Red Hen Press
Los Angeles, CA
www.redhen.org

Acknowledgements

Poems in the manuscript have appeared in the following journals and anthologies (sometimes in different versions or under different titles): "You Are Not the One Melinda Sings Her Underbreath Song to Please" in *Natural Bridge;* "Survival," "Born on This Place," "Taming Shad" and "Abstinence" in *Permafrost*; "Development of the Scientific Mind," "The New Hand on the Place Sets His Sights on Molly," "Dinah in the Bedroom" and "Conditions of the Sale" in *Torch*; "From the Unwritten Letters of Joseph Freeman" in *The Missouri Review*; "Sunday Morning" (first published in *The Los Angeles Review*) and *"and thou shalt be called a new name which the mouth of the lord shall name"* in *Evensong: Contemporary American Poets on Spirituality*; "The Truly Inhumane Act, or Kindness" in *Caven Canem VII;* "Almost Like They Wanted It" in *MiPOesias* and *Letters to the World: Poems from the WOMPO Listserv*; "She Liked the Moving Things Best" at *From the Fishouse*; "Code" in *Gathering Ground: An Anthology Celebrating Cave Canem's First Decade;* "At Madame Jane's" (sections 1 and 3) in *Pebble Lake Review*; "Pussy" in *New South*; *"Runaway* ran away" and "Dinah in the Box" (reprinted in *From the Fishouse* and in *The Ringing Ear: Black Poets Lean South*) in *The Mid-American Review*; and "Tis of thee, sweet land," in *Drunken Boat*.

"Almost Like They Wanted It, "Taming Shad," "At Madame Jane's," "Conditions of the Sale," and "Complicit" won the 2006 Dana Award.

The writing of many of these poems has been supported by fellowships and awards from the National Endowment for the Arts, the American Antiquarian Society's William Randolph Hearst Fellowship for Creative Artists, the Virginia Commission for the Arts, the Corporation of Yaddo, the Norton Island/Eastern Frontier Society, the Virginia Center for the Creative Arts, the Bread Loaf Writers' Conference, the Dana Award, Cave Canem, Randolph-Macon Woman's College, and San Francisco State University.

For their invaluable help in reading and responding to this manuscript, special thanks go to Shara McCallum, V. Penelope Pellizon, Jane Satterfield, Lauri Conner, Wendi Walters, Tayari A. Jones, Greg Pardlo, Shane Book, Matt O'Donnell, Alita Anderson, A. Van Jordan, Matthew Dickman, Major Jackson, Oliver de la Paz, Rick Barot, Sarah Messer, Rachel Flynn, Laura-Gray Street, Lucy Anderton, Michael Collier, Rebecca Brown, and Kathryn Dungy. For the shelter and support that helped make this book possible, I thank Mansah Prah, Cynthia Prah, Baby Prah, my amazing family, and Ray Black.

Contents

The Jennings House & Madame Jane's
Lynchburg, Virginia, 1842: Rebecca & Dinah

The Freeman House, Philadelphia
1831 – 1844: Melinda Freeman

When folks figure you are their slave, your past belongs to them.
And mind you, they might try to grab your future too.

—Ama Ata Aidoo

After the U. S. officially withdrew from the international slave trade, there remained three major ways to procure new labor to feed the country's ever-increasing appetite. New slaves continued to be smuggled from Africa, but resourceful traders turned to local sources as well. Domestic slaves were bred for profit and distribution, and kidnapped Blacks from Northern states were regularly added to the Southern lot.

Jackson Farm

Virginia

1831 – 1848

JOSEPH FREEMAN

The Trapper's Boast

Give me a crowd of colored men and I can spot the new arrivals—
freed men or fugitives—
I can tell them from those born with a claim to their flesh.

Runaways work to slip off a body's notice—
ring off a fattened finger—once again—

while the freed slave's desperate to be nothing more than a porter or carter—a man
meant to hold something most of the time.

I won't be bothered with fresh meat.

Just-from-slavery darkies are risky as rabbits just littered
—touch them and there's no telling what they'll kill.

Philadelphia's humid from new darkies' tears.

My mark is the colored man at ease with his freedom.

Give me a crowd of buckskins
and I will spot him too.

You are not the one Melinda sings her underbreath song to please

i.

You, Joseph Freeman, who once would sing words
the sermon could not say, the whole church waiting, Sundays,
for the Freeman song, and especially waiting for the bass cry
(such remembrance in your young body?) that was Joseph

Freeman singing in Meeting. You, Joseph, are not the one
who will sit in the men's pew singing, as you sang Sundays,
surrounded by your brother, your father, your uncle (Melinda,
your oldest friends, the whole church, maybe even the Good Lord

listening). No, Joseph, you are not the one whose back heat
and resting weight that pew's wood will curve and cup itself to welcome.

You are no more the one that pew's arch would recognize today
than you are the man who will hear, tonight, what new song Melinda,
in the rocking chair, (no more your rocking chair than her rooms are,
any more, your rooms) will catch under her breath and sing.

ii.

When you were Joseph, when you had two rooms
you could give your wife your hands and ears and mouth
inside, you listened. You let your wife keep you awake
trilling over what she'd cleaned that afternoon. *A cameo—*

her lips, a closed purse when she pronounced the m, opened for you
on the e, wider on the o—*strung on velvet.* You wrapped a band
around her neck, kisses, ending where the cameo would fall,
at the hollow, that perfect frame.

                                       When you had two rooms
and no one but your wife inside them, you could listen all night
to the things she desired. *Silk stockings,* for instance. What, you asked,
was wrong with the stockings she wore? *These wool ones?* You touched
the leg she lifted toward you. *I would be just as happy not to wear them
a minute more.* And didn't you listen to her? Didn't you
lend your hand and help Melinda peel those old stockings away?

iii.

Now you are a mouth tasting dust and salt and finger flesh.
You are all your remaining teeth arranged to satisfaction,
gums just pink enough to please. You are a saleable mouth
and your tongue does nothing. It does not curl into a consonant,
it does not shape the vowels that would add up to a plea
because you are not Joseph Freeman, night guard of Melinda.
The ones who wait on your voice are not the ones whose listening
would make a morning right.

                        Before you were nothing but an auctioned mouth
and a pair of hands that only mind commands, they made you
little more than a brine-sealed back and cross-hatched thighs.
Your tongue twisted in quick tempos as you learned
each new instrument's name: *cat-o-nine tails, pudding stick,*
ordinary oar. You'd rather keep silent than call up more cognates.
You, Joseph Freeman, who once would sing words.

From the Unwritten Letters of Joseph Freeman

Melinda, I've been preparing to write.
That peculiar girl named Molly,
who has a bit of liberty in the house,
has said she'll find some paper.
I have practiced mixing charred wood with water
and have managed to shave a twig
so one end nearly resembles a nib,
but tonight Lila got caught up
under the good Doctor's whip
for such a little offense. I am frightened.
Doctor Jackson brought in a new troop of slaves today.
A boy of thirteen among them had the welted cheek
that speaks of a driver's dissatisfaction.
Lila put a poultice on to ease the swelling,
but Jackson wants the boy to understand his place
and thinks a scar will help. Lila's back
and neck and arms have thirty new wounds
to replace the one she thought to heal.
Melinda, how is Jacob? Ever yours,

(February, 1841)

Do you ever start at night believing
I might be dead? I leave my body
sometimes, Melinda. Is that all dying is?
Remember how I'd scold you
when the stew was thin, believing
I needed a thick stock to forge muscle
for all the work I had ahead?
Your stew would make me big again, Melinda.
Sometimes we have to trap, skin and roast
possum, rabbit, snake and squirrel.
Except for that, I have swallowed naught
but salt pork and coarse meal in all my days
away from you. But I work just fine.
Ever your beloved husband,

What a herd of slaves Jackson brought in last month.
No sooner had their strength returned
after the long march to the farm from Lynchburg
but they began to plot another run.
We didn't know they'd planned to leave
until they were already gone a day.
All manner of neighborhood men
came around to tip Jackson's whiskey
and help him on the hunt, though
all they brought back for their trouble
were two bodies. One dead,
one fighting off living. That boy
I told you about, Ben with the slashed cheek?
At the stony fork of the river
Doc Jackson found his body, cut up,
twisted as if it had fought long
under water, a dead hand pointing
in the direction his netted sister and the "damned
lost lot of niggers" had run. I guess
he was too obstinate even for the water
to hold down easily. Jackson used Ben
like a scarecrow, his shirt hooked on a pole,
his body meant to warn us from the road.
Lila's still not certain that the girl will live.
Until tomorrow, I am ever your Joe.

(December, 1843)

William is the name Smythe matched
to my description when he shipped me
from his Wilmington slave pen
to the Richmond consigner Jackson
bought me from. So I am William,
though it took more than one whipping
for me to remember it.   There is a woman
keeps the kitchen here prefers we call her Auntie.
She's been called so many names
she "most forgets" which one means her.
I trust Jacob is getting on in school
just fine. I was, at his age, learning
to carry myself with the pride of a Freeman.
It's been many years since I've been able
to answer to any person calling me
that name. And Jacob? Can he remember
his father? Please hug him for me,
Melinda. I am ever your husband,

(November, 1845)

How many live on our alley in Philadelphia?
There, this room might accommodate
a bed and two chairs, but here we are three men,
two women, some potions, and a girl. We sleep
in turns. Marlo often walks the woods at night,
his eye out on the traps for all of us. 'Dolphus steals sleep
in the smithing shop and steals everything else
before dawn. Just last week, we bore the tread
of a muzzled goat and two hens he brought in
from a neighbor's farm. Our field sweat adds stench
to the store of bones, feathers, brews, and herbs
Lila claims can cure the women on this place.
Sadie, who Lila never tried to stop herself from bearing,
sleeps with her body wedged behind the door.
Molly swings it in her side each night when she turns up
to sleep after Miss Amy's laudanum takes and again
when she races the conch call to the house in the morning.
Even Lena, who had a well-built cabin of her own
when she lived on the place, pushed four babies off her tit
to make room for the Doctor and for Miss Amy's boy.
I wonder, Melinda, are your wages enough,
since I went away, to satisfy the rent? Yours in tribulation,

25

(December, 1847)

The Doctor's had his eye on Molly
since he caught her listening
while the tutor drilled his son on Greek.
She says the boy translates slowly.
On a war now, his spoiled tongue
has spent two days flogging
some warrior's impenetrable shield.
Molly showed me yesterday
what a heart looks like. Traced it
in the dirt that is my bed, my stool,
my desk, my cabin floor. I miss you, Melinda.
I miss feeling the little skip your heart took sometimes,
though I know the pinch that came along with the stutter
pained you. Molly is a smart girl,
though brutal in her zeal. She's quicker
than a butcher to find cause to wield a knife.
I am certain the Doctor will lapse in his vigilance
soon enough. Then I will chance to capture
on the page one of these letters. May God be good
and grant so large a prayer. Yours,

We are like to lose another hand
unless 'Dolphus can recover
from the flogging he took
over a missing pair of cufflinks.
The girl who was brought home
with Ben's body was quickly well enough
to work, and she had less skin on her bones
than Doctor Jackson left on 'Dolphus.
Perhaps there is some little hope
for Lila's husband. Molly is afraid
to sneak me any of the Doctor's paper.
Molly, who can be as bad as 'Dolphus
about purloining pretty, useful things.
I doubted she was earnest in her fear,
but now I see what she, born here,
must have always known. A man
whose livelihood depends on stealing
the toil of other people's bodies
must keep a keen eye on his own
most dear and precious things.

Survival

The body winnows. The body tills. The body knows
sow's feet, sow gut, night harvested kale. The body knows
to sleep through welted dreams, to wake
before the night succumbs to morning.

Wheat, wheat, tobacco, corn: the body knows.

No stopping. No sinking down. Like a branch
floats on water, the body does not go under.
Like a tree seeded among dark rocks, the body
leans where it must. Or fails.

Jackson Farm

Virginia

1848 – 1850

MOLLY & SHAD

Born on This Place

I had two sisters and a brother by my mother.
We buried the baby in the ghosts' grove, Mama counting
the pebbles her children tossed in: *One from Molly, two
from Hannah, three from Sol'.* When there was dirt enough
to keep rooting dogs from jawing her lost girl, Mama fed us
roasted shoat and sweet potato under a thieves' slim moon.

The month a milk cow shattered Mama's shoulder
and left her worth little more than a half hand,
Jackson threw in Sol' and Hannah when he sold her
to a trader came here on his way to Tennessee.

Didn't hurt him much to lose Mama and two quarter hands,
Jackson had raised his stock so well. They say
my father was the stud who worked this farm one week,
a wedding gift from the Missus' father to his newest son.
Twelve children born on this place in March of '33.

The Development of the Scientific Mind

The bones of the runagate, Ben, whom the Doctor ordered hung
then buried, were in due time dug up and delivered to him.

And the Doctor, on receiving Ben, scrambled, then ordered,
then hung him again. When Molly came with the draught
into the study, Ben's legs quaked. But he'd stopped running off.

Curious, Molly drowned a cat. With silver cutlery she returned before dawn,
she separated fat from viscera, seeking the blood source that compels a beast to run.

She allowed herself one page each time she dusted the Doctor's books, new volumes
ordered from England and the Continent. The books proved women distinct from men,
though nothing pictured explained why she was held apart.

Decoding each drawing with the keys she had gathered, she traced in dust
maps her rag would soon erase: the musculature of men, the dark, nested organs.

Molly could touch flesh and force change, but she was just the Doctor's girl.
Lila in the quarter did the herbs and birthing for the place. Few trusted Molly,
who kept close to Ben's bones all day when the Doctor went away.

After 'Dolphus caught her slicing into Marlo's roll-eyed, slavered, *Good Lord
still panting* pup, no one but the Doctor let Molly hold her quick hands near them anymore.

The New Hand on the Place Sets His Sights on Molly

Now they noticed

her body had wandered
into breasts and hips,

and through her sack cloth dress
they could sense the possibilities.

But before the other men had a chance to hold her body
in the dark circles of their eyes,

before they could lie down with the thought of her
against the contours of their minds,

before they could begin to figure how a week or a life
or whatever time chance and the woman granted

would redeem the sleep
they'd lose loving her,

Molly had become Shad's girl.

Sunday Morning

Desire swung like that: like her
legs in procession, like perfume
from a censer on its linked chain.
Heavy as smoke in the hold's light,
desire. A church, a cathedral, the body
in that robe. The robe sash swinging.
The progress through the sinning body
to this sacred spot. A man kneeling.
A man with head bent. A man lifting
his prayer to a woman. Desire. Desire. Desire.
Grant us grace.

The Truly Inhumane Act, or Kindness

When she was just two buds and a dream of sway
Molly had a hopethought that told her she would be someone
in whose presence men could try to be more than themselves.

But she's sixteen now.

                              She was in his arms
the night before, and because there was a moment
when the stroke of his grace overwhelmed her,
she is still there now.

                              And even now, barely a sleepthought
away from how Shad called her name to sound like settling down
in her was his left foot following his right foot into the craft
that would harbor him, Molly understands it is only his body
he needed to save and saving it, for her, had nothing to do with grace.

There will be nothing but hurt for days unless she reaches over
and, to the knots beside his spine, applies the plushpress of her thumbs
and soothing him that way grants some relief.

Taming Shad

Two things he didn't understand, even after
she let him pull her up into the wide hug
of the sycamore branches, and after
she took to tying her hair in red ribbons
he used Sunday wages to buy for her:
What had Molly's little nod meant that first day
her body, a bluebag gripped in one hand,
ran across his shadow? Laundry day,
so she was busy, but something made her take time
to answer a question he hadn't realized
he'd already asked. That was one thing
he couldn't understand. What made her
nod 'yes' to a dusty bruise of a man just walked up
to the Jackson place after how long trotting
behind his newest master and his master's paint?
The other thing was why, after all those nights
studying the creases in his thumbs,
the lobes of his ears, the direction sweat took
running off his belly, she stayed away from him
until the morning glories that had sprung open in his eyes
closed again. Did she have to remind him
wasn't nothing to be seen that he could look after?

Almost Like They Wanted It

Because she'd heard him laugh through new moon darkness
and she knew he'd fallen and she knew, before she turned,
he'd be crawling, like a crawdad, rock to loam—

because she tried to love the straight back and neck
he'd erected to recollect the man he'd been
before—because she found herself adding up his usefulness

like some kind of auctioneer—she showed him
the dark coils areoling both her breasts and all the ways
she bent and lifted, bent and lifted, steady, strong.

She let him believe he was past due for a harvest
and her hands were the right ones, now, to hold the scythe.

⁊

She made quick work of pleasure. The boysmile bunked down
in his eyes, she claimed. Her tongue found the place in his mouth
where the teeth were gone—where he'd hold his corncakes

until they grew soft enough to chew. History had bedded him
in all of this—his own history and failures not his own.
Before he'd tramped in she'd watched another man—a man she'd thought

she'd hated—watched his body opened, opened, opened until
blood had married brine. She'd watched that man be whipped into something
good for nothing more than fertilizing clay and she'd thought

buckshot would have been a brand of kindness if sprayed into him
just then. But even after his hard going, she did not miss him very much.

                                                  *

Anyone she chose could be shucked like surplus property tomorrow,
but that hadn't been enough to warn her off of picking him that night.
Because she knew if she set her sight on nothing she'd get nothing

in return, she'd walked with him. But because the night progressed so
—because there were some clouds—no stars—no moon—he'd tripped
over the branch of a dead and down tree. In all that darkness,

there, without a moon, even then, she had not fallen. She thought
to say so, but she did not say so. She did nothing
but say she was sorry for him. She did not use her mouth

to say this. Could he not listen to her hands? They spoke softly,
articulating her condolences, to his torn and bleeding skin.

Abstinence

Shad satisfied himself while Molly kept away
by thinking of the meat that had filled him up
one Christmas: roast turkey, duck,
peppered chicken wings, thick slices of salty ham.

The lady who ran the place Shad lived on part of '46
and most of '47 let her hands feast and dance two days
and gave them three more to recover—just think!
—before the heavy work resumed.

He shared a cabin that year with a man who cut himself
each morning. A man who'd been breaking his own skin,
an inch at a time, for seven years. Told Shad the cuts
drew feeling out and left it somewhere, harmless, on the floor.

That man ate nothing but potatoes and drippings,
even when offered game at the Christmas meal.
He told Shad, who lay still on his pallet, just thinking,
ain't a thing you'll hunger for, if you first refuse to taste.

She Liked the Moving Things Best

Molly didn't sleep the night she borrowed Master Fink's eye.
She knelt by the flat rock near her hold hole,
her belongings all around, and sent the glass eye clacking
toward the marbles, bumping the dice, wobbling, for hours,
the same direction the little blue ball rolled.

Molly couldn't help but be a little pleased by her courage,
showing the Missus' father's eye these things of hers:
the thimble, the silver fork—Miss Amy called it an oyster fork
when the set came up one short—the black button, the many
strings and ribbons, the brass cufflinks, the tiny glass vase.

Shad thought the collar button of his only buttoning shirt had fallen off
of its own accord. He believed Molly lost the pebbles and ribbons, the tokens
he gave her, thought she had too much on her mind most hours,
couldn't keep track of it all.

Shad thought Molly wanted the same things he wanted:
an arm crook to rest in before the conch call, a thigh
leaning against another's through the nighttime meal.

But Molly buried the things she liked best: the pinwheel
little Master Rufus left out in the yard, the red and yellow marbles,
the spinning top.

Aspire

August, and a lash of gnats is certain, prophesied.
Corn and wheat realize their ambition, while hands twist,
harvesting, through fields. Gnats
and heat and work songs engorge the clotted air.

Horses wear straw hats and join tree-shaded whipmen.
Everything they do is done with the sanctioned ease
of the master's favorite pup. The horses are absurd
with laughter as they watch the harvest's progress.

One summer dawning Shad will not rise. The vermin
and heat will light around him, the chant
of the tedious season will mark time, but he will be still
in the cool clay of his cabin. All he wants to be: still.

Code

Miss Amy wants me down to the market and see if I can't find fish *for sale. Two*
bushels to be delivered, but the driver's sick today. Miss hates to waste *house servants*
on errands, but we'll need the fish come dinner. Mostly scrod and she-crab(*the female*
be the best for my stew) is what I'm hunting for. Folks say I'm *not to be surpassed as a cook,*
the best girl round this place. Miss Amy claims she can't be bothered with another *washer,*
so today I'll see to errands, scrub clothes and stew fish, and tomorrow I'll be cook *and ironer too.*

Can't say as I blame Miss Amy her grip on the house. Heaven knows, *her husband's a first rate*
scoundrel, and a groggy fool to boot, they say master'd roll 'round the 'taters with a *servant*
girl name of Lena. Promised a kiss and a gold piece for some trick of the leg he saw *in a tavern*
in his bachelor days. Lena worked her whole life in this house. She ain't seen *and experienced*
enough to know to keep out of the cellar when the man's breath smells worse than *ostler's*
britches? Miss caught Lena's left arm, burned the thief's T in the thumb of her right *hand.*

Lesson

the child of the breast gets   *the child of the womb*

                                                        eats

the table served   the roasted meat   *scraps*
the savory pies

                                       the womb's child kneels and swallows

the child of the breast   knows   *hope only comes to the one who sucks*
       the best milk and claims the labor   *the marrow*
of working hours   *chews on the bone*

The Jennings House
& Madame Jane's

Lynchburg, Virginia

1842

REBECCA & DINAH

and thou shalt be called a new name,
  which the mouth of the Lord shall name

      ∾

     For Zion's sake I will not
      I will not hold my peace

  For Jerusalem's sake I will not

     I will not rest I will not
      I will not rest until the righteous go

      ∾

it was the roaming creature's birthright she was after
  so she marked the wanderings of a sick buck till it died

it was the wild creature's right to free death she desired

      ∾

the righteous go forth
  as the brightness the brightness

      the righteous go forth as the brightness and the salvation thereof

as the lamps that burneth

      ∾

  she marked the failing of a sick buck when it died
then stowed her traveling dress beneath the carcass

in three days she'd made a stench skirt   to slow the hounds
still more
        she polished her boots in his hide's rot
                                        sweet oil

℗

    and the Gentiles shall see   the Gentiles shall
    the Gentiles shall see thy righteousness   and all the kings
        shall see thy glory

℗

    she named herself Rebecca because that woman knew
            smell could run privilege out of a brute's tent
and secure it for the child she favored

℗

Thou shalt no more be called Forsaken
    neither shall thy land be termed Desolate

℗

        she was awhile preparing

but when she smelled most like disappearing

                                    she was gone

Dinah in the Bedroom

Dinah kept as still as she could, so as not to wake Jennings, while she considered

how she might rid herself of him. Last week, the girl who kept the kitchen disappeared.

Jennings had been in his cups the night before and didn't wake till nearly three that afternoon.

Dinah served him the bread and onion he prefers when his stomach's raw from brandy,

so it was the next day before Jennings called for Hepsie and nobody came. Not that girl

nor either of the kitchen girls he'd called Hephzibah before her. Jennings had no help now

but Dinah. She tried to pull away to use the slop jar, but Jennings, possessive even in sleep, gripped her

all the more fast around the waist. She didn't dare wake him with tonight's dose of amber fire

still burning in his belly. If she could trust herself to keep still she would cry,

but so long as Jennings kept her in his bed Dinah feared even her water

would be unable to escape.

At Madame Jane's

⤳

You'll be a platter for their cornbread
a skillet for their sauce
these city boys with dreams of country cunt

You will dust yourself in flour
if it's a dead nigger ghost they want

I tell you
yesterday I let two blistered brothers splay me like a dressed out doe

Boys with no more money than a chimney sweep will pay six days wages
to lay you under a felted whip

They reel in here off the river

They hitch themselves this deep into the Buzzard's Roost
then hop off of the train

They pay for promise in my house

Tell them, *Take me any way you want me*
(don't call them ugly)
you the boss man
you the one to show me what I need
(don't call them poor)

Got a judge comes here
first wet his loins inside a mammy looked enough like you

Burnt the last girl's hands when he bent her over the stove

I see to it the doctor tends her

She's been useless nearly two weeks
but I tell you
she still has her room
her herbs
and plenty food

It would cost an auctioneer the price of two good mules
to do you like he does girls everyday

A hand, a mouth, a pair of iron pincers come around your tongue
someone must of already paid

Take your dress off slowly if it suits you
I can charge them two bits just to watch a tit slip out the top

Got a doctor brings his son here so the boy can study how the inside of a woman moves

When you came here asking me for shelter were you shy?

No point in a nigger being shy

There's an auction outside the Congress Hotel this evening
remember
you been naked all your life
good for little more than breeding dirty dreams

I say it's time you see that profit
and that power

Remind me what you said that lawyer used to make you do

well then

you'll find the fellow waiting upstairs easy

He'll want to watch you take your supper from a chamber pot

I've stowed a clean one by the bed stand
Take this stew

I'll call you what I want
and the men will too

Hepsie
Hephzibah
Rebecca
girl
what makes you think you someone
worth a name?

Got a bed to sleep on
don't nobody come in less they pay

You only got to worry on that lawyer
or his brother
choosing you when they sober enough to recognize your new fat face

and don't nobody come inside this house I don't want in

Nothing else to worry 'bout
so you fretting over who to be today

Working here you're nobody and everyone

Best to forget you ever belonged to a body
could choose to answer to one name

Someone who love you call you Becca?
You want your past to track you now?

I burned the dress and boots you scuttled in here wearing

How many pair of boots I bring you yesterday?

Work for me a year you'll have money for a trunk of dresses
and a steamer ticket out of here
if you believe there's anywhere to go

I won't allow you to stay in my house
sounding out the letters of some missing slave girl's name

Pussy

I was once small as a shell among many shells,
black as a cowry's inner curve.

If I allowed the wrist-churn and tongue-lash
to break me, I would be no more than sand,
so much grit to wash off, ground to walk upon.

Soon enough they would find a way
to burn me up and look right through me.

These men, angular as filed teeth,
they would convert me to some thing
I would hate to recognize if I let them claim me,
that small and that expensive, as their own.

And so I made myself a stronger thing, a taut flash
of muscle wrapped bone. I am lean and quiet,
common as a mouser. These fools believe
they own me, because I paw through their houses
and eat what they can't stand.

Conditions of the Sale

Jennings' belly was a brandy barrel rolling over Dinah. She really must be Lena's child.

She remembers the haunt kiss of her mother's cool lips, that ghost

of a girl who had added four babies to the Jackson stock—the three boys were sold

for a neat profit—and was still no less pale nor any more firm of flesh

when her fifth pregnancy went wrong in some way that made her useless

to Jackson but all the more subject to Miss Amy. The cooper never built a barrel

so brutal as the one that Lena died in, nails jutting toward the core to test her corporeality.

What crime had Jackson attributed to her mother that day he gathered all the hands

to witness the breathing, beating-hearted Lena packed into the studded barrel

and rolled an acre down a hill? Dinah didn't know. But she did know

less than a week later Jackson started seeing Lena walking all around

the property. Miss Amy saw her too. She understood the haunting was Lena

finally finding a body to possess. While Dinah served the table, her skin looking delicious

as morning cream, or while she was bent to sweep the floor in Jackson's rooms, Lena was busy crowding the father's features out of the daughter's face. The buzzards weren't done

circling Lena's grave before Miss Amy had Dinah sold far off the Jackson place.

There Are Seven Things I Know,
And None of Them Is You

How to fast lace a boot
so the tongue is close.
So nothing is left loose.
So I can walk. So I can run.

How to run.

How to speak the words and numbers
that signify where I belong.
How to count the houses.
How to walk inside a room.
How to find the bed I'll sleep in.

How to know I am not home.

Runaway   ran away

       gone from *a* man claimed the *girl*
a man *named* the girl
      got the girl
          stored up in his room

              ↄ

             ran away
runaway
         gone
           Dinah   gone

              ↄ

                  19 years
          of age
      about five feet three inches
brown hair   a cask-shaped mark over her left eye

              ↄ

      no one *speaks*   no speech
        just hatching

              ↄ

           thought he knew her *well*
when she was in there with him
         not a word was *spoken*
      who *to* trust now?
thought he knew

              ↄ

         presents a gap
between her upper foreteeth when she smiles

Dinah in the Box

Dinah spent twenty hours with her face by the breathing hole, her body curled

like a nursing child's, wondering what order of thanks she would offer the man

who opened her crate. She had a particular trick that worked on Jennings

when she needed him to understand she meant to please, but Dinah wouldn't

be a bachelor's wench in Philadelphia. What angle would her legs take,

that first night in Philadelphia, in relation to the woman spot between them?

Not this infant's pose she was confined to now. Not any of the poses favored by Jennings.

What would her hands do, free to touch only what they chose? She had twenty hours

to remember every way she'd folded to get into this box. She'd tipped out extra brandy

until Jennings railed against the things he hated: taxes, drought, and abolitionists.

Turned out old Harrison, the carpenter, was suspected to be one. She tracked Harrison

and asked what price and means he'd name. Those two tasks proved more simple

than storing up the coins that slipped from Jennings' pocket to the rug beside the bed.

It took Dinah seven months to collect enough to buy the box and pay Harrison for the bill of lading. Dinah touched her knees, tracing the hinge inside them

that would straighten in some white man's parlor. She wasn't free yet, but soon

a man she would make herself trust would prize open the lid of her crate.

The Freeman House

Philadelphia

1831 – 1844

MELINDA FREEMAN

The House Book, or a Manual of Domestic Economy: Fuel, Fires, & etc.

Chapter I. Coal Scuttle

> *When the grate is entirely emptied, sweep it out clean with a hearth-brush, and...wash*
> *it out with a wet cloth. Remove the portable hearth from underneath, and empty the*
> *ashes into...an old scuttle brought for the purpose.*

I'm emptied, made heavy, emptied again, waiting
on the fire. Melinda Freeman. Joe was proud
to give his name to me. Hadn't been a slave

in his Daddy's line since '73. And both of us born
right here in Philadelphia. Seems to me, now,
it's no matter. If you're born black anywhere

you're most unlucky. A negro ain't nothing
but a thing to be used up. Being proud of a name
like Freeman. There's as much sense in that

as in trying to heat a house by burning ashes.

Chapter II. Grates and Stoves

What is called a perpetual fire, or such as many persons boast of continuing unextin-guished all winter, is wasteful of coal, and is never so bright and strong as that which is entirely renewed everyday, without the remains of the old fire.

The Committee met on Thursday to celebrate
safely conducting fifteen fugitives through our stations
to New York and then across the lake. Such a large group,
and still more were knocking before we adjourned.

I bring Jacob with me when the Committee gathers
in the evenings. He's at Clarkson's school on Locust
when I'm at Mrs. Cartwright's in the daytime, but at night...

his thighs are growing the same tensed muscles
that flexed his father's. I do not trust him to stay still
in the house while I am away. The Committee calculates
it has aided nearly two hundred men through Philadelphia
and on to Canada this year. All those legs running

through our houses. I'd held hope awhile, but I know
I should expect no news of Joe.

Chapter III. Hot Coals

If the dress of a female catches fire when she is alone, if she cannot extinguish it by squeezing it
in her hands, let her immediately ring the bell violently, or knock on the floor, but if possible,
avoid opening the door to run out, as admitting the air will increase the flame.

A gentleman just returned from Baltimore,
where his lodgings were adjacent to a slave pen,
spoke at our last meeting of these shambles:

the brick walls higher than the oldest elm
and thicker than a man's spanned hands;
the countless iron shutters;

the rowdies in the proprietor's employ
who make a practice of enticing men and boys from Philadelphia;
the coins exchanged for every body herded there—

so many, it seems, that they must take into slavery
more than all the anti-slavery committees
can take from it.

This is what we women gather to learn
after spending the day bent over boiling pots
of someone else's soiled laundry. This
is the information men collect to hear at the end of their laboring hours.

Where can our bodies rest and trust
that filth and tribulation will not overtake us there?

Chapter IV. Fire-Screens

In traveling on railroads, particles of cinder from the chimney of the locomotive frequently fly into the eyes of the passenger, causing intolerable pain...To avoid these painful and sometimes dangerous accidents, ladies should always travel with veils, holding them closely down over their faces.

Met a woman today thought she'd shipped herself
off of harm's door porch. You're just free of Virginia,
I scolded. She couldn't read, so I showed her
one of the caution placards the Committee has taken to posting
and told her what it said. What this girl loved best was to walk
without pass or purpose and then return home
to her own bed. Mind yourself, I cautioned,
pointing toward the scruffed man who'd started
lurking at the grocer's corner. He fit the description
of the scoundrel the handbill suggested might be bent
on stealing any colored person he could get a hold of.
Signs all around: curtains drawn, women not hawking,
no men with picker's shoulders to be seen
even on this laborers' street. I saw the sun eclipsed
the year Joseph was taken and was a fool to be surprised
by the sudden absence of a face that marked each moment
of my day. Watch yourself. Or head on up to Canada,
I told her, if you're set on wandering in such an aimless way.

Ring Hand

The nail of the thumb I dropped the stew pot on purpled,
died and, years ago, grew back, awkward now, twisted.

This son of mine, my Jacob, was just a toddling boy
the day I lost hold. I was readying myself
to prepare the meal, expecting Joe back from the butcher,
when Sally Turner came, instead, supposedly to comfort me.

Joe is tall and lean and skilled at laying brick. A man like him
would fetch a good price in Virginia. Had my thumb healed correctly?
My hand would bear no mark, but Joe would still be slaving.

Jacob is dreaming of marriage. He covers his stained pallet
every morning, but I know. He'll be gone in a blink of years.

Still, I can remember nursing him, and I can remember,
because he could not be kept away, Joe sitting by me.

I'd let him hold my hand, kiss the palm and every finger.
I'd smile a wife's smile when he confessed how he loved me
and to prove it sucked my thumb into his mouth and held it,
our communion, against his lips and teeth and tongue.

Complicit

"We'll have to round up all these free men and send them back to Africa." *Friends*
of Mrs. Cartwright's, Colonization Society folks who think she ought to *be informed,*
say Liberia is waiting. They ask, "What other way?" They ask what other chance *there is*
for the colored race to hope for true improvement.

Mrs. Cartwright says, for her part she's glad to know I'll always be *on hand*
in Philadelphia. Quick as it's said, I'm sent to market for *common width calicoe*
I'll sew into work frocks for her in-house girl *and fine shirting muslin*
from which I'll fashion shirts for all the little Cartwright men.

A year into Joe's absence I burned my petticoats, flannels, *all of*
Jacob's trousers. I couldn't let the skin he touched touch *cotton*
and wouldn't let my mouth wet rice. I ate nothing sugared, *cultivated*
a taste for boiled water so I could wean myself from tea.

My employer looks to Rev. Finney to learn which acts will prove her faith. She gets *by*
quite alright since Mr. Cartwright's textile ventures have begun to do so *well*
(she told the ladies who came today for coffee). Her help is handsomely *remunerated*
to assure loyalty (she added after I'd removed myself and all their untouched cakes).

The production of sugar for a family of five requires several months' *labor*
from one slave. I still eat little but greens, tubers, beans and fruit. *The free goods*
my grocer sells. I suffered through summers in wool *and*
owned no kerchiefs until the Committee opened a free *labor store.*

Observation on the Return of Migratory Birds

I record each arrival. Early and late
the birds are returning. The blue jay, March 1.
Pigeons and robins, the week before my birthday.

I am only here, in this last week of April, seeing chickadees

wing back and gather nesting. I need the eye I am
when I am witnessing this small and songful resolution,
feathered collations ledge-perched, tufted shadows

skimming our alley's cobbles and then gone

and then back again. When these flitters return
to my block of the black ward one morning and stay
on into the evening, always, I notice, I smile.

Unravel and Weave

When I hang Mr. Cartwright's trousers on a line
with no thought as to how the leg would taper down Joe's calf,
I am nothing more than myself, and happy
to be Melinda Young, now Freeman.

But, of course, I am no longer Young,
and no more Freeman than Hattie down the alley,
whose old man, Elijah the porter, went off
ten years since with another gal, is a Porter's bride.

Because there has been no dirt turned over
the body I love, because the hands that stole
my plans were neither death's nor some other
seductress, because I have no body to blame,
no betrayal to explain my kidnapped ambition,
there are moments I can do nothing but forget
I must be someone's widow, someone's abandoned wife.

It is difficult to answer if I am more or less myself
in the late evenings when I take calls from men
like Richard Turnbridge, who would have me drop Freeman
and fold myself into his name.

                    And who am I
when I am waiting on the corner? Just Melinda,
watching for a break between the carts and carriages,
wondering, only, when the time will come
when it is quiet enough for me to walk into the road.

Turnbridge

Richard is flesh that answers questions,
each limb real as furniture,
and he has brought us to a house with many rooms.

Thirteen years is too long for a boy to only know his father by a broadside.
Richard has taken Jacob up and is teaching him a trade.

We are harboring a young man who confiscated himself about a month ago.
He's no more than 16, but his master is eager to pay
as much as twelve hundred dollars to get him again.

He said no old men lived on his last place.
Only a few worn-out women.

Men past their prime were sold at cost,
he said, if they weren't already dead.

He'll tell Richard more, but I've moved on
to the next chore, in a different room.

Three men to feed and clean behind, all their woolens to darn
and trousers to mend, there's hardly time
for all I must attend to every evening.

Two days ago, I forgot until this morning, was Joseph's birthday.
His thirty-second.

Lord bless his body
if he lives.

'Tis of thee, sweet land
  (a poem of found text)

I tremble for my country when I remember God is just.

∽

keep a sharp look out
      under trap doors or in attic crawl spaces

50,000 fugitives found shelter
not far from where they took a glass of brandy

pistols and bowie knives
suddenly become scarce in the market

the padlock and chain were left in the woods

∽

raised corn and cotton and cane and 'taters and goobers

then along came a Friday and that a unlucky star day

we have been at some great pains to ascertain the facts

∽

the institution is destined to become extinct
at some distant day
the wells have in some places dried up
and the supplies of many mill streams have been much reduced

the public are hereby cautioned against trusting or giving credit to any person

about Richmond
the locusts abound
they have cast their old shells and are depositing their eggs

they have been heard to say blood must be shed

Primer, Or A History of These United States (Abridged)

A fiction based on fact: The characters and narratives in **Suck on the Marrow** are fictional, true to the reality of how history proceeds. As the circumstances and sites depicted in our history are inspired by actual documents and facts (many of which are cited and glossed in the following pages), any resemblance to real people or events is not the least bit coincidental.

A half hand: Slaves were often listed in sale advertisements, deeds, and other registries according to their worth: a half hand, like the one mentioned in **"Born on This Place,"** would be worth half the going rate of a fully able-bodied worker, a quarter hand worth 25 cents on the dollar, and so on.

A blue bag: Perpetual access to the contents of this household requirement might be worth more or less than a slave, depending on how much you value your linens. A blue bag, like the one mentioned in **"Taming Shad"** was a bag of bluing substances, usually derived from anil or indigo, used to brighten white fabrics that have yellowed in the wash.

"Aspire": Like so much of history, this version was inspired by another's. "After Tomas Tranströmer," is how many books would phrase this fact.

Auctions: One way to move human property was through slave auctions such as those referred to in **"You are not the one Melinda sings her underbreath song to please: iii"** and **"At Madame Jane's."** Newspaper advertisements were another common method of alerting potential buyers to impending sales. The italicized text in **"Code"** is from a sale advert reproduced in *The Emancipator and Journal of Public Morals*, October 21, 1834. Slaves of high value to a household might yield a greater profit in a sale—imagine a slave who was particularly intelligent or specifically skilled, or consider women who bore a number of healthy slave children and also served as milk nurses for legitimate sons. With or without their families, these slaves were often the first assets liquidated. Less costly replacements could usually be found.

"and thou shalt be called a new name, which the mouth of the Lord shall name": We've done what we can to create sense out of chaos (see *chaos*), but the order's all mixed up. We understand. Very little

in history is alphabetized, truly chronological, or logical. Consider the Bible: The italicized text here is from Isaiah 62: 1-4 from which verses come the definition of the name Hephzibah: "the Lord delighteth in thee." Consider the hunt: Just as bird dogs are taught to ignore other animal's scents, well-trained slave hounds were taught to track human scents and ignore other trails. Consider the hunt in the Bible: In Genesis 27, Rebecca uses animal skins to lure the master of the house, who loved wild game to distraction, into fulfilling her will.

"At Madame Jane's": What became of Rebecca? This is all we know: "The 'Buzzard Roost' neighborhood in Lynchburg was well known for its gambling houses, bars, houses of prostitution and other 'dens of iniquity.'" It was a neighborhood, common to many larger towns and cities, where populations of runaways "thrived." So claimed *Free Blacks of Lynchburg, Virginia, 1805-1865* researched and written by Ted Delaney and Phillip Wayne Rhodes. They knew that history is at once an open book and a blind alley.

Books: **"The House Book, or a Manual of Domestic Economy: Fuel, Fires, & etc."** was published in 1840 by Miss Eliza Leslie of Philadelphia. A handy little text (both the book and the resultant four-chapter poem), the former proved a resonant source of inspiration and information, including all titles, subtitles, and epigraphs recorded in the latter.

Chapters: Dungy's **"The House Book, or a Manual of Domestic Economy: Fuel, Fires, & etc."** is divided into several chapters including **"Chapter II. Grates and Stoves,"** which references Anti-slavery committees such as Boston's New England Anti-Slavery Committee, founded in 1832, and the Philadelphia Vigilance Committee (1838-1844) which flourished in Northern cities in the 1830s and 1840s. Local vigilance committees provided necessities such as clothing, food, board, medicine, money, transportation, start-up support, and legal assistance to fugitive slaves. Organizations and their members operated despite great legal, personal, and material risk. On May 14, 1838 the ornate Pennsylvania Hall opened in Philadelphia to house the American Anti-Slavery Society. This building was irreparably burned as a result of riots on May 17, 1838. Appreciating the desire to achieve their integrated goal, but equally aware of many such dangers inherent in ignoring the strength of individual units, chapters were meant to function both independently of and in concert with the main. In **"Chapter III. Hot Coals"** there is direct reference to an article called "From a speech of Mr. George Thompson to the Rochester Anti-Slavery Convention," published first in *The North Star*, April 10, 1851. Abolitionist newspapers like *The Liberator*, first published on January 1, 1831, *The Emancipator*, and *The North Star*, informed disparate organizations of the movement's collective progress and kept the fire of abolitionist vigilance alive.

Chaos: On February 12, 1831 the major solar eclipse mentioned in **"Ring Hand"** passed across Eastern North America striking many as a sign of doom and sparking a variety of disastrous event**s.**

"Complicit": The italicized text in this poem is from "Free Labor Store, 376 Pearl Street," an advert posted by Joseph Pearl in *The Emancipator and Journal of Public Morals,* July 22, 1834. Purveyors like the Free Labor and Temperance Grocery Store, founded in Philadelphia in 1834, provided goods and materials to those who, in recognition of their call for Immediate Abolition, refused to take part in any aspect of the slave trade. On the contrary, the American Colonization Society understood the immediate value of the slave system while pursuing the long-term goal of gradual emancipation. Their hope was that the bulk of America's free colored population would eventually be removed to settlements in Africa. When the American Colonization Society was founded in Philadelphia in 1817, three thousand members of the free colored community gathered in protest.

Delaware: One of the northernmost states below the Mason-Dixon line, through which slaves like Shad (last accounted for on Jackson Farm in Virginia) might have been bought or sold (see *auctions*) to points further south (such as Baltimore or Richmond) and other, perhaps luckier, souls might flee northward into Philadelphia, New York, or even Canada (see *Dinah*).

Dinah: Born in 1823 to Lena (d. 1836) who was recorded as the property of Doctor Jackson of Jackson Farm, Virginia. Dinah was sold to a Mr. Jennings who resided in the city of Lynchburg, Virginia in whose house she remained until records lose her in 1842. It is suspected that she made her way through Philadelphia, assisted by one or more vigilance committee members.

Earthquake: February 7, 1812, a forceful earthquake struck the city of Philadelphia and its environs.

F-K: As with any history, some information has been omitted from this record.

Lost: Explore your local library for *A Registry of Births, Deaths, and Unions of Those Without Record.*

Melinda: (Young, Freeman, Turnbridge, etc.) Born the year of the Philadelphia tremors (see *earthquake*) and married to Joseph Freeman, born the same year. Their son, Jacob, was born in October of 1828. After his birth Melinda returned to her job as a domestic in the home of the Cartwright family of Philadelphia. Following Joseph Freeman's disappearance in 1831 (see *chaos*), Melinda became active in a vigilance committee (see *chapters*), and by August of 1843 entered a binding, legal contract with a fellow member of the organization.

Molly: A fish popular for home aquariums, bred in a variety of colors, especially black. A young girl registered as the property of Doctor Jackson and serving his wife, Amy Fink Jackson, and only legitimate child, Rufus. A diminutive of Mary. In one version, a wild woman or a female companion of ill repute. Sea of bitterness.

None of the above: (see *lost*).

"Observation on the Return of Migratory Birds": This title and the dates herein were borrowed from handwritten notes made in a Philadelphia edition of *Poor Robin's* Almanac, 1833. Bless these scribbles in the margins.

P-S: Bless them.

"'Tis of thee, sweet land": Title from "America," Samuel F. Smith (1832); epigraph, Thomas Jefferson as quoted in the *American Anti-Slavery Almanac*, 1837; line 1 from "Caution!! Colored People of Boston...," a placard written by Theodore Parker, April 24, 1851; line 2 from *Underground Railroad Conductor*, Tom Calarco; line 3 from *A Pictorial History of the Negro in America* by Langston Hughes and Milton Meltzer; lines 4 and 7 from "Just from Slavery," *The North Star*, February 27, 1851; lines 5 and 6 from "Boston, 21ˢᵗ," *The North Star*, February 27, 1851; line 8 from "Mary Reynolds, Texas," in *Unchained Memories: Readings from the Slave Narratives*; line 9 from "James Green, Texas" in *Unchained Memories: Readings from the Slave Narratives*; line 10 quoted from the *Commercial Advertiser* of July 5, 1834 in *The Emancipator and Journal of Public Morals*, July 22, 1834; lines 11 and 12 from a letter by Henry Clay quoted in The Auburn *Coon Killer*, September 6, 1844; lines 13, 14 and 16-18 quoted from *The Richmond Compiler* in The Cooperstown *Freeman's Journal*, June 5, 1826; line 15 from an advert in The Cooperstown *Freeman's Journal*, January 18, 1830; line 19 quoted from the New York *Commercial Advertiser* of June 9, 1834 in *The Emancipator and Journal of Public Morals*, July 22, 1834.

U-Z: (see "*Lesson*")

Biographical Note

Camille T. Dungy is the author of *What to Eat, What to Drink, What to Leave for Poison* (Red Hen Press, 2006), a finalist for the PEN Center USA 2007 Literary Award and the Library of Virginia 2007 Literary Award. Dungy has received fellowships from organizations including the National Endowment for the Arts, the Virginia Commission for the Arts, Cave Canem, Bread Loaf, the Dana Award, and the American Antiquarian Society. Dungy is an associate professor in the San Francisco State University Department of Creative Writing. Editor of *Black Nature: Four Centuries of African American Nature Poetry* (University of Georgia Press, 2009), she is co-editor of *From the Fishouse: An Anthology of Poems that Sing, Rhyme, Resound, Syncopate, Alliterate, and Just Plain Sound Great* (Persea Books, 2009) and assistant editor of *Gathering Ground: A Reader Celebrating Cave Canem's First Decade* (University of Michigan Press, 2006). Her poems have been published widely in anthologies and print and online journals.